Dinosaur Story

by Joanna Cole

Illustrated by Mort Künstler

SCHOLASTIC INC.

New York Toronto London Auckland Sydney

To Kathie and Amy

The author and artist wish to thank Dr. Eugene S. Gaffney, of the American Museum of Natural History, for checking the manuscript and illustrations for the first edition of this book. They would also like to thank Michael Brett-Surman, of George Washington University, for checking the manuscript for the revised edition of this book.

ISBN 0-590-43348-2

12 11 10 9 8 7 6 5 4 3 2 1   9/8 0 1 2 3 4/9

Printed in the U.S.A.   23

Under the ground, something is buried.
Inside the rocks, something is hidden.
It has been there for millions of years.
What is it?

It is a bone. The bone of a giant dinosaur.
Scientists want to get the bone.
They chop into the rocks with pickaxes.
They dig up the bone.

Tyrannosaurus rex skeleton

The scientists find many bones.
When they put the bones together,
they have a dinosaur skeleton.

Dinosaurs lived millions of years ago,
long before there were people on earth.
So we can never see a live dinosaur today.
But dinosaur skeletons help scientists find out
what dinosaurs were like.

This dinosaur was very big.
It was longer than a trailer truck.
It was heavier than ten elephants put together.
It was so heavy that every step it took
must have sounded like thunder.
Because of this, scientists named it Brontosaurus,
which means "thunder lizard."
Today this dinosaur has a new name.
It is called Apatosaurus.

Apatosaurus

For a long time, many scientists thought Apatosaurus
stayed in the water almost all the time.
They thought the giant "thunder lizards" swam
in rivers and swamps and ate soft water-plants.

But now scientists think
these dinosaurs lived on land.
They think these huge animals
ate leaves and bark from trees.
No one knows for sure.

These dinosaurs may have
stayed together in herds.
When they ran, the smallest dinosaurs
stayed in the middle of the herd.
The biggest dinosaurs ran on the outside
and protected the small ones from enemies.

Allosaurus

Allosaurus was the enemy of Apatosaurus.
It was not as big as Apatosaurus.
But it was fierce and quick.
It had strong arms and sharp claws.
Its mouth was filled with sharp teeth.
Allosaurus did not eat plants. It ate meat.
It killed Apatosaurus and other dinosaurs for food.

But it was not easy for Allosaurus
to kill *this* dinosaur.
This dinosaur was well protected.

Stegosaurus

Its name is Stegosaurus,
which means "covered lizard."
Stegosaurus's back was covered
with large, pointed plates.
On its tail were four long, sharp spikes.
It was hard for Allosaurus
to make a meal of Stegosaurus.

Ornitholestes

At the same time that these dinosaurs lived,
there was a smaller dinosaur, the size of a man.

Its name is Ornitholestes,
which means "bird-robber."
Bird-robber was fast enough to catch birds.

In those days, birds looked different from
the birds we know today.
On each wing they had three claws.
And they had sharp teeth in their beaks.

They could fly from tree to tree,
but they could not fly as far as birds can today.

Ornitholestes

At the same time that these dinosaurs lived,
there was a smaller dinosaur, the size of a man.

Its name is Ornitholestes,
which means "bird-robber."
Bird-robber was fast enough to catch birds.

In those days, birds looked different from
the birds we know today.
On each wing they had three claws.
And they had sharp teeth in their beaks.

They could fly from tree to tree,
but they could not fly as far as birds can today.

If a bird landed on a low branch of a tree,
bird-robber could jump up and catch it.
But sometimes the bird was too fast.
It might climb up the tree,
using its wing-claws to grab onto branches.
Or it might fly to another tree.
When this happened,
bird-robber could not catch the bird.

Then bird-robber would eat other things.
It would eat insects, small lizards, and mammals.
It would even eat the eggs of other dinosaurs.

The first dinosaurs lived on earth
for millions of years.

Then, very slowly, they began to disappear.
Apatosaurus died out. Allosaurus died out.
All of the first dinosaurs died out.

But at the same time,
new kinds of dinosaurs appeared.
They took the place of the earlier dinosaurs.

Protoceratops was one of the new dinosaurs.
It was a plant-eating dinosaur.
It was not a giant.
It was only five or six feet long—
about the size of a small pony.

Protoceratops

All dinosaurs hatched from eggs.
But the eggs of Protoceratops were
the very first dinosaur eggs ever found.
Scientists found whole nests of Protoceratops eggs
buried in rocks.

The scientists think many mother Protoceratops
laid their eggs together in the same place.
The mother dinosaurs dug holes
in the sand to make nests.
Then they laid their eggs
and covered the nests with sand.
They did not sit on their eggs
the way a chicken does.
The mother dinosaurs were too heavy for that.
They left the eggs in the sand.

Protoceratops

All dinosaurs hatched from eggs.
But the eggs of Protoceratops were
the very first dinosaur eggs ever found.
Scientists found whole nests of Protoceratops eggs
buried in rocks.

The scientists think many mother Protoceratops
laid their eggs together in the same place.
The mother dinosaurs dug holes
in the sand to make nests.
Then they laid their eggs
and covered the nests with sand.
They did not sit on their eggs
the way a chicken does.
The mother dinosaurs were too heavy for that.
They left the eggs in the sand.

The sun warmed the eggs.
Fresh air came through the sand.
The sun and the air helped the eggs hatch.

When the eggs were ready to hatch,
they began to move.
Tiny dinosaur beaks pecked at the eggshells.
Here and there a baby Protoceratops
popped out of the nest.

At first the babies were small.
They were only the size of rabbits.
But they would grow.
In time they would be as big as their mothers.

Ankylosaurus

Styracosaurus

Protoceratops was only one of the new dinosaurs.
There were many others too.
A few of the new dinosaurs, such as Ankylosaurus, had armor.
Some had thick plates on their bodies.
Some had sharp horns and spikes.

Triceratops

Triceratops was the biggest
of the horned dinosaurs.
It was as big as a car.
It had a bony shield on its head and neck.
And it had three sharp horns.
That is why it is named Triceratops,
which means "three horns on the face."

Tyrannosaurus rex

Triceratops was a plant-eating dinosaur.
It walked along the edge of the forest.
It ate leaves and small plants.

It needed its horns to protect itself
from Tyrannosaurus rex—"king of the tyrants."

Tyrannosaurus was taller than a two-story house.
It had big jaws and many, many teeth.
Each tooth was six inches long.
Tyrannosaurus could eat almost every other dinosaur.
It was the most terrible dinosaur there ever was.

Often Tyrannosaurus ate duckbilled dinosaurs.
Duckbills were large. They were as tall as Tyrannosaurus.
Their bills were shaped like the bills of ducks.
Their front feet were webbed like ducks' feet too.
Duckbills lived on land.
But they sometimes swam in the water and ate water-plants.

Duckbills

Duckbills stayed together in a herd
to protect each other.
When they were in a herd,
Tyrannosaurus could not catch them.
But if one duckbill got lost
or could not keep up with the herd,
Tyrannosaurus could catch it.

Tyrannosaurus ate very fast.
It tore off big chunks of meat
and swallowed them whole.
But sometimes it did not eat fast enough.
Sometimes another Tyrannosaurus saw it eating.

The other Tyrannosaurus tried to get
the whole duckbill for itself.
It came running. It showed its teeth.
It tried to chase the first Tyrannosaurus away.

But the first Tyrannosaurus would not go.
It would not give up its food.
It stayed and fought back.

What a battle that must have been!
Two giants running and dodging.
Two sets of teeth snapping and biting.
Two enormous dinosaurs fighting to the death!

Millions and millions of years went by.
Then all the dinosaurs died out.
One by one they died, until there were
no more dinosaurs left anywhere.

Why did the dinosaurs die out?
There may be many reasons.
Maybe the weather changed.
Or the marshes where they lived may have dried up.
Perhaps the plants changed,
and the dinosaurs could not eat them.
No one knows for sure.

Big and small, plant-eaters and meat-eaters,
armored dinosaurs and horned dinosaurs—
all the dinosaurs disappeared.
Today all of them are gone.
Only their bones are left to tell their story.